OPERATION OUCH!

Medical Milestones and Crazy Cures

Dr Chris van Tulleken
and
Dr Xand van Tulleken

LITTLE, BROWN BOOKS FOR YOUNG READERS
www.lbkids.co.uk

LITTLE, BROWN BOOKS FOR YOUNG READERS

First published in Great Britain in 2014 by Little, Brown Books for Young Readers

A CIP catalogue record for this book
is available from the British Library.

ISBN 978-1-4055-2981-5

Typeset in Arial by M Rules
Printed and bound in Great Britain by Clays Ltd, St Ives plc

Papers used by LBYR are from well-managed forests
and other responsible sources.

MIX
Paper from
responsible sources
FSC® C104740

Little, Brown Books for Young Readers
An imprint of
Little, Brown Book Group
100 Victoria Embankment
London EC4Y 0DY

An Hachette UK Company
www.hachette.co.uk

www.lbkids.co.uk

Contents

Introduction 1

The Brain 7

The Eyes 23

The Nose 35

The Mouth 51

The Ears 75

The Skin 85

The Hair 109

Blood and the Heart 125

The Lungs 145

The Limbs 157

The Stomach 167

The Bladder 181

The Bottom 193

First Aid Tips 207

INTRODUCTION →

WELCOME TO OPERATION OUCH!

CHRIS: Hi! I'm Doctor Chris.

XAND: And I'm Doctor Xand.

CHRIS: And we're going to take you back through time.

XAND: Like that other famous time-travelling doctor, I'll be helped out by my companion, Chris.

Chris

Xand

CHRIS: Actually, YOU'RE the companion, Xand. Everyone knows that.

XAND: Er . . . fine. We'll be visiting a time before clean hospitals and anaesthetic.

CHRIS: When it was not so much Operation Ouch as Operation AAAARRRRGGGHH!

XAND: You'll be glad you were born this century as you learn about the bloody, pus-stained medicine of the past.

CHRIS: Did you know, for example, that just a couple of centuries ago, a doctor would have sliced into your skin and drained your blood to try and make you better?

XAND: Many of the weird treatments we'll be looking at are from the days before medicines were properly tested, and before the body was fully understood.

CHRIS: And some of them are VERY weird. People used to think, for instance, that drinking your own wee was a great way to stay healthy.

XAND: Hmm, nice! Along the way, we'll be looking at some heroes of medical history, too, and sharing some amazing body tricks that will astonish your friends.

CHRIS: So roll up, roll up! For the medical history tour, step right this way . . .

XAND: We'll be starting with the most important bit of all – your brain.

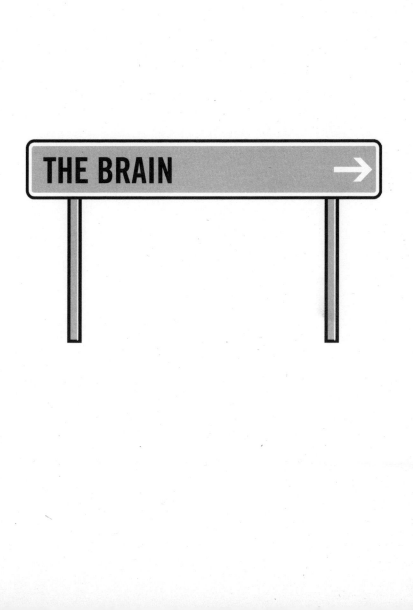

CHRIS: Tense, nervous headache?

XAND: Yes.

CHRIS: Why not try drilling a hole in your head?

XAND: Er . . .

CHRIS: It's called 'trepanning' and it used to be a popular treatment.

Trepanning was practised for thousands of years. Holes have been found in skulls that are over seven thousand years old, making it one of the oldest medical practices we know about.

There are records of trepanning in Ancient Greece, Rome, Egypt, China and many other civilisations. In some traditions, the bone was scraped away with a sharp stone such as a flint – ouch! – while in others, tiny holes were drilled in the shape of a circle so a fragment of skull could be pulled out. Double ouch!

Trepanning was used to cure headaches, seizures and sickness – none of which sound as bad as trepanning itself – as some cultures thought these problems were caused by evil spirits trapped inside the skull.

CHRIS: The hole was meant to let them out . . .
but it might have let even more evil spirits in.
It could have turned into an evil spirit party in
there . . .

In 1965 a Dutch man called Bart Huges tried to
revive trepanning. He was convinced that the
amount of blood in the brain controlled health, and
that popping a hole in your head would do you a
world of good. To prove it, he made a hole in his
OWN skull with an electric drill and went around
telling everyone how brilliant it felt.

XAND: I think I'll just have a nice lie down instead.

CHRIS: If you've ever had a bad headache, you might have felt like your brain was throbbing in your skull.

XAND: But it's not your brain itself that's hurting, it's the bits around it such as the blood vessels. The brain itself can't feel pain.

CHRIS: Many peculiar cures for headaches have been suggested over the years.

XAND: Some of them are so weird that just thinking about them can give you a headache.

In the Middle Ages, eating walnuts was suggested as a cure because they resembled the head. This came from the idea that God had made plants and herbs that looked like the body parts they could cure. So if you find a potato that looks exactly like a famous footballer, say, you might be able to use it on him next time he's injured.

A book written in the ninth century called *Bald's Leechbook* recommends tying a plant called 'crosswort' to your forehead with a scrap of red cloth (how annoyed would you be if you only had blue cloth in the house?), while a tenth-century Arabic cure involved binding a dead mole to your head.

XAND: Imagine it: 'Try dead mole for fast-acting relief!' – and funny looks from everyone you walk past.

Electric eels were used for headaches in Ancient Rome and South America. One crazy version suggests touching one hand to the eel and the other to the forehead. Sounds like nonsense? But did you know that recent trials have shown that electrical pulses might help with headaches? Maybe they were on to something! So why not keep a few live eels in your medicine cabinet? Even if they don't cure your headache, they'll give your dad a fright, which will give you a laugh.

CHRIS: That's a terrible idea, Xand. Really, don't.

XAND: In the nineteenth century, our understanding of the brain was helped by a gory accident.

In September 1848 an American railway worker called Phineas Gage was blasting rocks when a long, iron rod fired through his left eye and out of the top of his head.

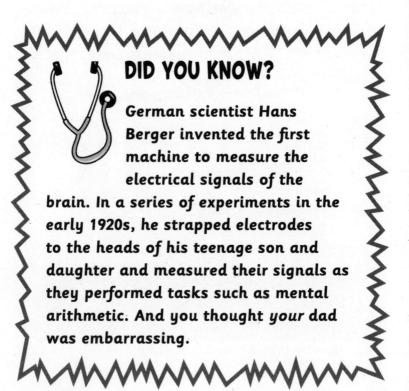

DID YOU KNOW?

German scientist Hans Berger invented the first machine to measure the electrical signals of the brain. In a series of experiments in the early 1920s, he strapped electrodes to the heads of his teenage son and daughter and measured their signals as they performed tasks such as mental arithmetic. And you thought *your* dad was embarrassing.

CHRIS: Now that's got to sting.

Gage survived, but his personality seemed to take a turn for the worse. According to a report written after his death, he was hard-working and popular before his accident, but became bad-tempered and rude after it. He even started to swear in polite company.

Warning: do NOT try and use this as an excuse to be rude to people. You do not have a steel pole sticking out of your head.

He was immortalised in a popular poem:

> A moral man, Phineas Gage,
> Tamping powder down holes for his wage
> Blew the last of his probes
> Through his two frontal lobes
> Now he drinks, swears and flies
>   into a rage.

His story changed the way we think about the brain. It led many to believe that different parts of it control different parts of our personality. It also proved it was possible to recover from very

 15

serious brain injury, which influenced the treatment of patients with similar problems. Both Gage's skull and the metal rod are now on display at the Harvard Medical School in America.

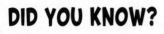

DID YOU KNOW?

The first ever medical journal in English was published in 1684 and was called 'Medicine Curiosa or a Variety of New Communications in Physick, Chirurgery, Anatomy, from the Ingenious of Many Parts of Europe and Some Other Parts of the World.' Despite the snappy title, it only lasted a couple of issues.

Heroes of Medicine:
Nicholas Culpeper

In the seventeenth century, snooty English doctors published their works in Latin so ordinary people couldn't snoop at them and work out how to make themselves better.

A doctor called Nicholas Culpeper changed this by translating directories, such as the *London Pharmacopoeia*, into plain English. It helped thousands of people who could never have afforded doctors.

These days, websites such as NHS Choices and utterly fantastic TV shows like *Operation Ouch!* bring medical knowledge to millions.

QUIZ

Where did the Ancient Egyptians think intelligence came from?

A. The brain
B. The heart
C. The bottom

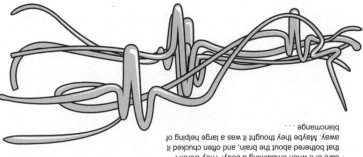

The answer is B: They thought the heart was the most important part of the body and took special care of it when embalming a body. They weren't that bothered about the brain, and often chucked it away. Maybe they thought it was a large helping of blancmange . . .

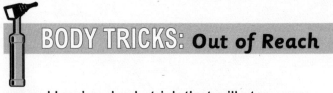

BODY TRICKS: Out of Reach

CHRIS: Here's a body trick that will stop your friends picking things off the floor.

XAND: First find something that's very precious to them.

CHRIS: For example, if I were playing this trick on Xand, I'd use his teddy bear, Mr Grumbles.

XAND: Don't drag Mr Grumbles into this. That's crossing a line!

CHRIS: Tell them to stand against the wall and place the precious item in front of them.

XAND: They'll try and bend down to pick up their beloved item, but they won't be able to.

CHRIS: This is because when you bend over, your body adjusts itself backwards for balance. But it can't do this if you're flat against a wall. You have to look on helplessly at the precious object, unable to reach it.

XAND: Or you could flop forward on to the ground and cradle your precious object.

CHRIS: That might work if it's a teddy bear . . .

XAND: Hey!

CHRIS: But not if it's a model of the Houses of Parliament made out of matchsticks, for example.

XAND: Your eyes are a very precious part of your body.

CHRIS: They bring you wondrous sights like sunsets, rainbows and this book.

XAND: As well as not-so-wondrous ones like multi-storey car parks, puddles and dog poo.

CHRIS: No wonder we've been so obsessed with keeping them healthy throughout history.

One scroll found in Ancient Egypt suggests pig eyes mashed with honey should be poured into the ear as a cure for eye problems. Another recommends tortoise brains mixed with honey.

Crazy as these might sound, the Ancient Egyptians may have been on to something with one of the ingredients. Research has shown that honey can help kill bacteria. If only they'd realised the honey was doing all the work, it might have been better for all those poor pigs and tortoises!

Another cure was dabbing bats' blood in the eyes. You can see the idea: bats have good eyesight, so surely their blood would help improve our eyesight? Sadly, this one was complete nonsense. Bats' blood won't make you see better, cheetahs' blood won't make you run faster and dogs' blood won't make you bite the postman and chase after sticks.

If the part of your eye called the 'lens' goes cloudy, you'll have trouble seeing. This is known as a 'cataract' and many cultures have worked out you can treat it by removing the lens. An account from tenth-century Persia suggests cutting a hole in the eye, sticking a hollow tube inside and sucking the lens out. It says you need someone with extraordinary lung capacity to do it. Hopefully not too extraordinary, though – you wouldn't want to suck out their brains, too.

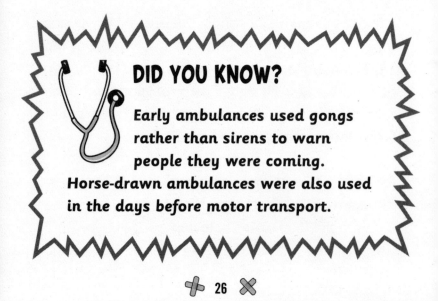

DID YOU KNOW?

Early ambulances used gongs rather than sirens to warn people they were coming.
Horse-drawn ambulances were also used in the days before motor transport.

CHRIS: One treatment for eye problems is so common we take it for granted.

XAND: Millions of people around the world keep specially-shaped bits of glass attached to their face at all times.

CHRIS: In other words, glasses.

XAND: Before their invention, there wasn't much you could do if your eyesight went blurry.

CHRIS: At least it was before the invention of television, so you wouldn't have had to miss *Operation Ouch!*

In the Middle Ages, a monk called Roger Bacon discovered that certain shapes of glass could help with sight problems. The earliest glasses were developed in Italy in the thirteenth century.

Some initial designs were rather strange. Early versions had to be held up by handles, meaning you had to choose between poor vision and tired arms, while others were shaped like scissors and worn on a ribbon or chain around the neck. Remarkably, it wasn't until the eighteenth century that modern glasses frames, which fit over the ears, were invented.

XAND: Come on, guys - the ears are just around the corner from the eyes! Why didn't you think of it sooner?

This was great news for cool people later in the eighteenth century when dark glasses were invented. Before then, they had to sit around looking moody to let you know they were cool.

Heroes of Medicine: Maggots

Unlike some of our medical heroes, maggots have never been awarded any prestigious prizes, and no one has ever built statues of them. But they deserve to be celebrated all the same.

Maggots have been used as a medical treatment by cultures such as the Maya Native Americans and the Australian Aborigines and, amazingly, they're still used today.

If you put maggots on a wound, they'll eat away the dead flesh but leave the nice new flesh, allowing it to heal. It's a win-win situation: humans get rid of the

IN LOVING MEMORY OF
LORD MAGGOT

dead flesh that could otherwise lead to infections, and maggots get to scoff their favourite meal. Yum!

So let's build a statue of some maggots. They deserve it, and it would look cool.

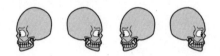

QUIZ

What medical instrument did René Laennec invent using a piece of paper in 1816?

A. The scalpel
B. The stethoscope
C. The dialysis machine

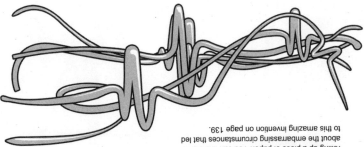

The answer is B: he created a stethoscope by rolling up a piece of paper. You can find out more about the embarrassing circumstances that led to this amazing invention on page 139.

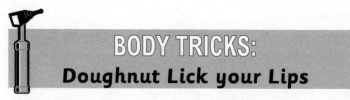
CHRIS: This must be the most enjoyable body trick ever.

XAND: All you have to do is eat an entire sugary doughnut without licking your lips.

CHRIS: Think it sounds easy? Try it.

XAND: You almost certainly won't be able to, and it's because of the sensory receptors in your lips.

CHRIS: Your lips have more receptors than pretty much anywhere else, so they're sensitive to things like sugar.

XAND: As soon as they feel something irritating them, they tell your brain to remove it.

CHRIS: And that's why you can't resist licking your lips.

XAND: So the next time your parents catch you scoffing a doughnut, tell them you're performing an important scientific experiment.

CHRIS: That excuse will probably only work once, though. You can't tell them you need to repeat the experiment every day just to make sure.

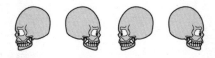

DID YOU KNOW?

It was once believed that birthmarks were linked to wishes that hadn't come true during pregnancy. For example, if a woman craved strawberries but didn't eat any, her child would be born with a mark resembling a strawberry.

THE NOSE

CHRIS: The nose is . . . *sniff* . . . affected by . . . *sniff* . . . one of the most common . . . *sniff* . . . illnesses in the world . . . *sniff* . . . which is . . . *snort* . . . the common cold.

XAND: Can you stop doing that, please?

CHRIS: I'm just . . . *sniff* . . . reminding everyone . . . *sniff* . . . how irritating . . . *sniff* . . . colds can be.

XAND: You've reminded me, and I'm irritated. Now stop.

The common cold is a viral infection of the nose, throat and sinuses. It causes sneezing, coughing and horrible snot to go everywhere. There's no cure for it, though simple medication can help.

The Ebers Papyrus from Ancient Egypt recommends a mixture of fragrant bread and the 'milk of a woman who has borne a son', along with a spell that begins, 'Spit it out, thou slime, son of slime.'

CHRIS: We now know, however, that you can't get rid of a cold just by insulting it.

Even that wasn't as odd as the cure in Ancient Rome. The writer Pliny the Elder recommended drinking jaguar wee and eating hare poo. He believed that illnesses such as colds were caused by demons and these horrible things would drive them away. In truth, it wouldn't drive the cold away, but it would have driven all your friends away.

An Arabic text from the Middle Ages blames cold weather. But this leaves the author wondering why some people catch colds in summer too. His explanation is that the heat causes part of the brain to melt and flow out of the nose. He recommends wearing a hat.

A medical book in the eighteenth century reckoned colds were caused by poison in the air that mixed with your saliva before you swallowed it. The solution was to spit all the time.

Disclaimer: Spitting is horrible and people in the eighteenth century only recommended it because they were bonkers.

DID YOU KNOW?

A medical book from the ninth century lists a disease called 'elfsickness', which was thought to be caused by invisible elves shooting tiny arrows into people. The cure was a drink made from a plant called 'dwarf elder'. Either it wasn't a very reliable book, or *The Lord of the Rings* was a documentary.

Strange though these old remedies might be, we can't scoff too much at them. After all, we STILL haven't found a cure for the pesky cold virus all these years later.

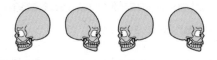

XAND: Did you know that nose jobs are thousands of years old?

CHRIS: This is the name for a type of surgery where someone gets their nose re-shaped.

In Ancient India, noses were replaced with skin from the cheek or forehead. This skill was in great demand, because criminals often had their noses lopped off for punishment. Techniques such as this weren't adopted in the western world until centuries later, when Italian surgeons looked for ways to treat the facial wounds of soldiers.

These early nose jobs were used for people who had lost or wounded their noses, but the practice of reconstructing perfectly healthy noses only developed in the late nineteenth century. Now an entire industry of cosmetic surgery caters for those who are unhappy with their physical appearance.

CHRIS: As well as wanted criminals trying to disguise themselves . . .

Needless to say, it's much better to learn to love your nose than spending time and money replacing it with a new one.

XAND: In 1772 a man called Joseph Priestley stuck something up his nose that would have a massive effect on the world.

CHRIS: His finger?

XAND: No. It was nitrous oxide, soon to become known as 'laughing gas' because it makes you giggle.

Although laughing gas was invented in 1772, it wasn't used as an anaesthetic until the middle of the nineteenth century. Think of all those poor patients who could have been helped if someone had thought of it sooner.

An American dentist called Horace Wells volunteered to try laughing gas at a circus in 1844. He noticed its numbing effect and wondered if it could be used for something more than making carnival crowds chortle. He tried to demonstrate its anaesthetic properties to a crowd in Boston, but muddled it up and was booed off. It would be another decade of painful tooth-yanking before everyone realised he'd been right all along.

Another American dentist called William Morton demonstrated that a gas called 'ether' could also be used as an anaesthetic, and this one was strong enough for serious surgery as well as dentistry. Soon patients all around the world were breathing ether before operations, and hospitals became less fearful places.

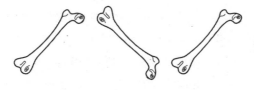

DID YOU KNOW?

Someone who sells fake goods is referred to as a 'snake-oil salesman'. The expression comes from the travelling salesmen who used to claim their useless oils were miracle cures for all sorts of things. They would even plant people in the crowd to say they'd been helped by the bogus medicine! The travelling doctor became a stock character in Westerns. They ride into town, sell as much of their rubbish stock as they can, and leave before everyone realises it doesn't work.

Heroines of Medicine:
Florence Nightingale

Florence Nightingale was born into an upper-class British family in 1820. She wanted to become a nurse, even though her posh parents thought it was beneath her. Hospitals were grim places back then, filled with the cries of hapless patients being operated on without anaesthetic, so you can see why her parents weren't keen.

Florence made her name in the Crimean War, which was fought between Russia, Britain, France and Turkey from 1853 to 1856. Florence was sent with a team of military nurses to improve conditions for wounded soldiers. And conditions needed improving, to put it mildly.

Military hospitals were filthy and overcrowded, with rats lounging around in puddles of blood and diarrhoea, and beds so full that many patients had to lie on the floor. Even if you had survived the gruesome battlefield, you might not survive the stinky hospital.

Nightingale introduced amazing new ideas, like not putting patients on the floor in puddles of blood and poo. She was known as 'The Lady with the Lamp' because she made her rounds at night with a candle lantern (you'd have wanted one too, with all those rats around).

There's no doubt that Nightingale helped to lay the foundations for modern nursing, though some think we should pay as much attention to other figures from the same period, like Mary Seacole (see page 69).

BODY TRICKS: Getting Stuck

CHRIS: This body trick will stop your friends from standing up straight and leave them trapped in an awkward position.

XAND: First, get them to stand facing a wall and fold their arms across their chest.

CHRIS: Then get them to bend over until their head touches the wall.

CHRIS: Then get them to take a step back, while keeping their forehead against the wall.

XAND: Now tell them to straighten up again. They'll find they can't.

CHRIS: It's because their centre of gravity will have shifted when they took a step back. Their weight shifted to their head, and their tummy muscles aren't strong enough to straighten up.

XAND: They'll be stuck, and you'll be free to use them as a piece of furniture.

CHRIS: Think of it as not so much losing a friend as gaining a bookshelf.

DID YOU KNOW?

Warts are caused by human papilloma viruses, but they were once thought to be caused by witches. Bizarre cures included rubbing coins on them, or chopping the head off an eel and smearing the blood on them. Please don't try any of these!

XAND: Chris's breath is smelly! Chris's breath is smelly!

CHRIS: We begin our look at the mouth with the sensitive subject of bad breath.

XAND: Chris's breath is smelly! Chris's breath is smelly!

CHRIS: Most people will be too embarrassed to tell you if you're suffering from it.

XAND: Chris's breath is smelly! Chris's breath is smelly!

CHRIS: Except for your brothers and sisters, of course. They'll absolutely love telling you about it.

Have you ever suffered from bad breath? If someone you spoke to winced, and you weren't standing on their feet, you might have done. Amazingly, bad-breath cures go back centuries. We're talking about the days before sewers, when everyone threw poo and wee out on to the street – how could anyone smell stinky breath over the top of all that?

In Ancient Egypt, a mixture of cinnamon, myrrh and honey was swallowed to combat bad breath. In Rome, the writer Pliny the Elder suggested gargling with wine before bed every night, while the medieval French writer Guy de Chauliac believed rabbit's blood was the best thing.

CHRIS: That's right. He thought breath could be improved if it smelt like a dead rabbit. What on earth must it have smelt like before?

In the early twentieth century, the term 'halitosis' became popular thanks to an advertising campaign for a mouthwash. The ads gave stinky breath a medical name that made it seem like a serious condition.

GROSS OUT

Being accidentally buried alive must be one of the worst things that could ever happen to you. In the nineteenth century, when Edgar Allen Poe was writing horror stories about people who woke up to find themselves trapped in coffins, the world got into a panic about premature burial. Corpses were checked for signs of revival by tickling them and stuffing things down their throats. A device called the 'safety coffin' was even invented, to help the 'accidentally buried'. It contained a pulley system with a bell for getting attention if you ever found yourself waking up six feet under.

As the large amount of ancient cures show, humans have never been very fond of rotten breath. These days it's a serious no-no, and you'll be cast out of polite society if you forget to brush your teeth for a week, or burp in someone's face right after eating a Scotch egg.

XAND: Now that we've cleared up that breath of yours, you can open wide so we can look at your teeth.

CHRIS: We all know that toothache can drive us crazy. So maybe it's fitting that so many cures for it have been utterly mad.

An Ancient Egyptian papyrus recommends curing toothache by putting a dead mouse in your mouth. It probably didn't stop your teeth from hurting, but at least the disgusting taste of rotting mouse would take your mind off it.

The Ancient Egyptians and many other cultures thought toothache was caused by small worms burrowing into the teeth. They believed the tiny creatures could be flushed out with hot water, or smoked out with candles and hot beeswax. Sometimes the entire tooth was removed as a cure for toothworm, and some even believed the exposed nerves underneath to be the worms in question, and attempted to yank those out, too. Ouch!

A similarly strange cure in Ancient Rome involved rubbing your mouth with a hippopotamus tooth and eating the ashes of a wolf. Roman school children would no doubt get in massive trouble for going to bed without hippopotamus-toothing their teeth.

XAND: And some people complain about having to brush their teeth every day!

CHRIS: But it stops them getting fillings and blasting everyone with morning breath.

XAND: And it's a lot easier than it used to be. In the past, you'd have had to use a twig instead of a toothbrush.

In Babylonian, Chinese and Arabic cultures, twigs were chewed to clean the teeth. They were free,

 58

didn't need toothpaste and it didn't matter if you ever forgot your toothbrush as you could simply find a tree and break off a new one. As long as you removed the ants first.

The first toothbrushes were made in China out of the bristles from pigs' necks. These bristles must have done the trick, because they were still being used in toothbrushes until the 1930s, when they were replaced with nylon. Thanks for helping us brush our teeth all that time, pigs!

Toothpaste can be traced back to the Ancient Egyptians, Greeks and Romans, though the ingredients were very different back in those days. They used things like crushed bones, charcoal and eggshells.

XAND: And nothing fills your mouth with freshness like crushed bones, charcoal and eggshells.

DID YOU KNOW?

An American doctor in the early twentieth century called Henry Cotton became convinced that mental illness could be cured by pulling teeth. He took out thousands of gnashers in the hope of curing the infections he thought caused mental problems. He even took out some of his own. A visitor to his hospital found it very disturbing, because everyone had difficulty eating and speaking.

Believe it or not, charcoal toothpaste wasn't the worst flavour in history. During World War Two, a toothpaste called 'Doramad' contained the massively dangerous metal, radium. It claimed it would turn your teeth white and shiny but didn't mention it could also give you cancer. This is because the health risks of radium weren't understood until decades after it was discovered. And so, for the only time in history, people who forgot to brush their teeth were actually doing themselves a favour.

CHRIS: If you have a problem with your teeth these days, you can pop along to the dentist.

XAND: You'll visit a nice, clean surgery and be given anaesthetic to take away any pain.

CHRIS: What you won't get is crowds swarming around to leer at your agony.

XAND: Yet this is what would have happened if you'd visited a medieval tooth puller . . .

From the Middle Ages to the nineteenth century, tooth pullers plied their trade at markets and fairs. They'd wear necklaces made from teeth and perform a bizarre mix of dentistry and entertainment.

And as if that wasn't terrifying enough, they'd often be assisted by clowns playing musical instruments. It all sounds like a horrible nightmare.

Some teeth were so rotten they could pull them out with their fingers, but others required a device called 'the pelican'. This was shaped like a pelican's beak, and looped around teeth to wrench them out with a lever. Pelicans weren't as accurate as today's dental tools, and they sometimes ripped away the gums and surrounding teeth, too. But they were still a better option than leaving rotten teeth in the mouth.

While it might have been embarrassing to have your teeth pulled out on stage, it helped drum up business. Large crowds were drawn by the clowns and music, and if the tooth man could show off his skills, many of the crowd would step up to have their own diseased molars pulled out. As long as the music was loud enough to drown out the screams of agony, it was a good advert for the tooth man.

CHRIS: If you don't look after your teeth, you could end up having to wear false ones.

XAND: These days, dentures are made of plastic and fit neatly into your mouth, but they weren't always so convincing.

The Ancient Etruscans made dentures from the teeth of animals such as oxen. It can't have been very comfortable to have their massive teeth in your mouth, and you probably felt like a cannibal whenever ox burger was on the menu.

Elephant tusks were also sometimes used to make false teeth. They were carved into the shape of human teeth, though – people didn't just strap entire tusks to their gums and try to chew food.

Human teeth were used to make dentures in the eighteenth century, but they were difficult to get hold of. One way was to pay the poor to have theirs taken out, but even the most desperate would need a lot of convincing to part with their precious gnashers. Another way was to steal them from corpses, so for some bodysnatchers (see page 136), teeth became a profitable sideline.

CHRIS: Dig up a corpse, sell the body to a doctor and flog the teeth to a dentist . . . what a lovely job. Their parents must have been so proud.

Porcelain dentures were developed in the late eighteenth century. They were much more effective and didn't involve having the teeth of dead people in your mouth and being totally disgusting.

Modern dentures are made from plastic and based on a mould of the patient's mouth. They might not be quite so good as the real thing, but they work much better than ox teeth.

XAND: Going further back into your mouth, we find your tonsils.

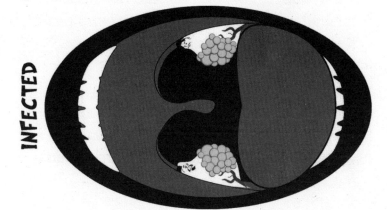

INFECTED

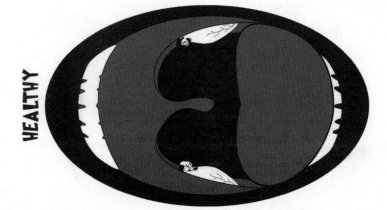

HEALTHY

CHRIS: Nobody knows exactly what tonsils are for, but we do know they become very painful if they swell up.

XAND: This is known as 'tonsillitis'.

CHRIS: Getting your tonsils taken out these days is very simple, but you wouldn't want to have gone through it in the Middle Ages . . .

A surgeon in tenth-century Persia described a gory process for removing the tonsils:

1. Get the patient to sit facing the sun with their mouth open.

2. Get a servant to grab the patient's head.

3. Get another servant to hold the patient's tongue down.

4. Twist a hook into the tonsils and stretch them forward.

5. Chop them off with scissors.

6. Try to ignore the patient's cries of agony and the look of wide-eyed terror on their face.

Things got slightly better in the nineteenth century with the invention of the 'tonsil guillotine'. This scary metal implement was shoved into the patient's mouth to slice their tonsils off. Although it was an improvement over hooks and scissors, the tonsil guillotine caused heavy bleeding, and died out as modern surgery developed.

DID YOU KNOW?

As part of a study to see how the muscles in the face control expressions, nineteenth-century French doctor Duchenne de Boulogne found a way to make one of his patients smile. He attached electrical probes to his face to control his expressions. Seems a lot of effort – couldn't he just have told him a joke?

Heroines of Medicine: Mary Seacole

The number of people that can be remembered from certain periods is limited – if it weren't, history lessons would last for ever and it would never be time for lunch break. But, sometimes, interesting people deserve to be discovered again.

We've all heard of Florence 'The Lady with the Lamp' Nightingale and her efforts to improve hospitals in the Crimean War (see page 45), but another nurse from that era, Mary Seacole, should be remembered too.

Mary Seacole was born in Jamaica in 1805 to a Caribbean mother and Scottish father. She learned medicine from her mother as well as from British military doctors.

When the Crimean War broke out in 1853, Seacole offered to join a group of nurses heading out to help but was rejected. Not being put off, she went by boat and opened her 'British Hotel', a metal hut in which she tended wounded soldiers.

Seacole was mostly forgotten after her death in 1881, but a campaign has brought her good deeds to light again. These days, 'Mother Seacole' takes her place alongside 'The Lady with the Lamp' in the history of Crimean War nurses.

QUIZ

Why is the anaesthetic nitrous oxide known as 'laughing gas'?

A. It gives out a high-pitched giggling noise when released
B. It makes you laugh if you inhale it
C. It was invented by Sir Horace Laughing in 1844

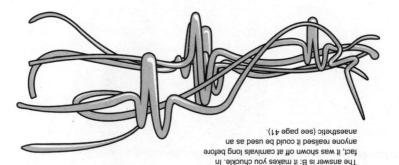

The answer is B: it makes you chuckle. In fact, it was shown off at carnivals long before anyone realised it could be used as an anaesthetic (see page 41).

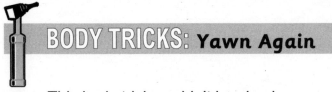

BODY TRICKS: Yawn Again

CHRIS: This body trick couldn't be simpler.

XAND: All you have to do is yawn in front of your friends and then watch as they do the same.

CHRIS: No one is quite sure why yawning is so contagious.

XAND: Some people think yawns help us to take in more oxygen, keeping us more alert and awake.

CHRIS: So yawning in groups helps everyone stay more vigilant.

XAND: Others think yawning was a way early humans communicated tiredness so they could co-ordinate sleep times.

CHRIS: Whatever the reason, yawning next to your friends will most probably make them yawn too.

XAND: You might even have yawned while reading this page, as just thinking about yawning is enough to set some people off.

CHRIS: In which case, stop it right now, or everyone will think this book is boring.

XAND: We should never have brought the subject up in the first place, come to think of it . . .

CHRIS: Your ears are very delicate and sensitive.

XAND: And we don't just mean those flaps of skin on the side of your head that hurt when people flick them.

CHRIS: Those are just your outer ears. You also have middle ears and inner ears.

XAND: Damage to these can cause hearing loss, and all sorts of bizarre treatments have been suggested for this.

These days, problems can be treated with things like hearing aids and cochlear implants, but before the workings of the ear were fully understood, solutions tended to be rather random.

Hundreds of traditional cures for hearing loss involved stuffing herbs, fats or even twigs into the ear. One of them even recommends pouring boiled wee in there.

XAND: Which is weird in several ways. Firstly, who agreed to have wee poured in their ear to find out if it worked? And secondly, who boils their wee anyway?

An American doctor in the nineteenth century recommended getting struck by lightning. He told the story of a deaf boy who could hear perfectly again after being struck in the ear. However, many doctors at the time were touting lightning as a miracle cure for all sorts of problems, including blindness and cancer. Let's hope not too many people followed their advice and rushed outside in storms, hoping to get zapped.

A medical reference book at the end of the nineteenth century recommended the 'carbolic smoke ball'. This was a rubber ball that released acidic smoke with 'healing powers' into the nose. It wouldn't have helped your ears and would probably have been horrible for your nostrils, too.

CHRIS: Some periods of history have been especially perilous for the ears.

XAND: And we're *not* just talking about the day Justin Bieber released his first single . . .

CHRIS: Many of the soldiers who survived the First World War came home with serious injuries.

XAND: And one of the most common types was hearing loss . . .

When the First World War ended in 1918, thousands of soldiers came home deaf, or with massive hearing loss. This was caused by them experiencing the unbelievable noise of the guns and bombs. Some of the explosions were so loud they could be heard all the way over in England, from France.

The loudness of noise is measured in decibels, and experts agree that prolonged exposure to a noise of 85 decibels or more will damage your hearing. Explosions in the First World War measured over 140 decibels, and gunshot could measure as much as 150. No wonder so many soldiers had their hearing damaged.

The only way most soldiers could protect against these noises was to stick their fingers in their ears, which couldn't stop shockwaves of pressure bursting their eardrums. These days, soldiers are given ear protectors as part of their kit.

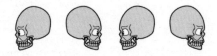

DID YOU KNOW?

The fictional detective Sherlock Holmes was based on a surgeon at the Edinburgh Royal Infirmary called Joseph Bell. Arthur Conan Doyle was a student of his, and was inspired by Bell's method of working things out from the tiny details of a patient's appearance.

QUIZ

What bodily function couldn't American waitress Lucy MacDonald stop herself doing between 1963 and 1965?

A. Burping
B. Farting
C. Hiccupping

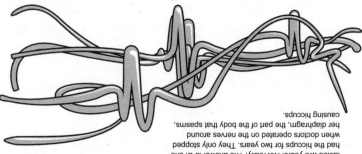

The answer is B: she did a continuous fart that lasted two years. Not really. The answer is C: she had the hiccups for two years. They only stopped when doctors operated on the nerves around her diaphragm, the part of the body that spasms, causing hiccups.

BODY TRICKS: Zombie Arms

XAND: This trick will make your arms rise up all by themselves, as if you were a zombie.

CHRIS: First, stand in an open doorway with your arms by your sides.

XAND: Then push the backs of your hands against the sides of the doorframe as hard as you can for a minute.

CHRIS: Then walk out of the doorway and try to relax your arms.

XAND: If you've done it right, your arms will start rising up of their own accord.

CHRIS: This is because your arms were pushing so hard, it takes your brain a while to realise the force has gone.

XAND: The muscles on the outsides of your arms stay tense, lifting your arms up.

CHRIS: Leaving you shuffling around with your arms raised like a zombie.

 83

XAND: Unlike zombie arms, however, they won't rot and fall off.

CHRIS: I'm sure that will come as a relief if you've just tried the experiment.

CHRIS: From the smallest nick to the largest gash in the skin, doctors have always tried to heal wounds.

XAND: This is the part where you start to feel REALLY glad that you live in the era of clean hospitals and anaesthetic.

CHRIS: Get ready to wince. And not just at Xand's jokes.

XAND: Oi! Speak for yourself!

Ancient Egyptians had some very weird cures for wounds. A scroll dating from 1500 BC suggests treating them with the fats of a lion, hippopotamus, crocodile and snake.

CHRIS: Which is handy, as you'd have had quite a few wounds after trying to collect fat from that lot.

The same scroll recommends filling head wounds with powdered ostrich egg and shouting, 'Repelled is the enemy that is in the wound! Cast out the enemy that is in the blood!' The idea was that one of the Egyptian gods such as Isis would hear you and cure the injury. But only if you'd used ostrich

egg. Nothing annoys a god more than rubbing the wrong type of egg into your head.

CHRIS: The Middle Ages weren't a great time to need a doctor.

XAND: Unlike today's doctors, medieval surgeons weren't concerned with making things easy for patients.

CHRIS: Quite the opposite, in fact. The Middle Ages were truly the golden age of ouch.

French surgeon Henri de Mondeville believed patients should suffer as much pain as possible. He thought ordinary, uneducated people wouldn't trust doctors who spared their patients, and would view them as weak and inexperienced.

The poor patients of medieval surgery had to suffer unbearable pain, long before the invention of anaesthetic. Their cries and struggles were so upsetting that onlookers sometimes fainted and injured themselves, which only meant more work for the surgeons. Ker-*ching*!

To stop them struggling, patients were either strapped to wooden planks, held down, or had their feet tied to their necks. Surgery often went wrong, and doctors made sure they were paid in advance so they could escape angry relatives. If there were any left that hadn't fainted, that is.

CHRIS: In the eighteenth century, a new method of treating wounds was developed.

XAND: It was different. It was radical. It was completely mad.

CHRIS: Believe it or not, doctors thought it would be a good idea to treat the *weapon* that caused the wound, as well as treating the wound itself.

GROSS OUT

Some medical books were bound in actual human skin. You can see the logic – they'd dissected the corpse to write the book, so they might as well use the skin to bind it. A small book on display in the Surgeons' Hall Museum in Edinburgh is bound in the skin of a famous murderer: William Burke murdered sixteen people with his accomplice William Hare in the early nineteenth century (see page 137). Being turned into a pocket book was part of his punishment.

'Weaponsalve' was an ointment applied to swords, axes, lances or whatever else had caused the wound. If the original weapon couldn't be found, the ointment could be applied to a wooden replica and it would still work just as well (in other words, not at all).

The Swiss writer Paracelsus described a way of making weaponsalve that involved mixing turpentine, linseed oil and blood with moss scraped off the skull of a hanged thief. When all these unlikely ingredients were gathered, they were to be mixed in a mortar and smeared on the guilty weapon.

CHRIS: Or you could have smeared it on your own bottom for all the good it would have done.

Let's hope weaponsalve doesn't make a comeback any time soon. It would be incredibly annoying to get kicked out of hospital so that your bed could be used to treat the car that knocked you off your bike.

XAND: In the Middle Ages, doctors didn't just treat wounds. They created them.

CHRIS: This was the golden age of 'cautery', which is the polite term for poking patients with red-hot irons.

Cautery was used to stop heavy bleeding, especially after amputations. And it worked – a scalding bit of metal applied to a wound can stop bleeding. But medieval doctors couldn't leave it there. They used cautery for everything.

Many doctors recommended it even if you didn't have anything wrong with you, as they believed it helped with general health.

XAND: That must have been awkward at check-ups: 'The good news is that you're perfectly well. The bad news is that I'm going to torture you with this smoking hot iron.'

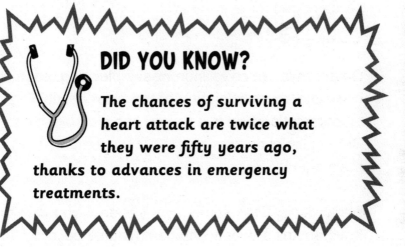

DID YOU KNOW?

The chances of surviving a heart attack are twice what they were *fifty years ago*, thanks to advances in emergency treatments.

Medical books from the time give detailed instructions about which bit of the body to burn to treat particular illnesses. One of them even comes with a helpful warning that if you cauterise someone's head for too long, their brains will start to cook. You can see the problem – not only will the patient be damaged for ever, but the doctor will be made hungry by the delicious, sizzling smell.

CHRIS: While we're examining skin, we're going to have to mention one of the most horrible diseases in history.

XAND: The bubonic plague was a disease that caused rashes, fever and 'buboes', which were painful swellings under the skin.

CHRIS: It was a deadly, destructive disease, killing millions as it swept around the world.

XAND: And if you went to see your doctor, you'd find him dressed as a scary crow.

One of the most famous outbreaks of the bubonic plague was known as 'The Black Death'. It reached Britain in 1348 and went on to kill between a third and a half of the population.

 94

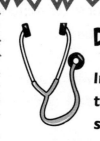

DID YOU KNOW?

In the Middle Ages, it was thought the skin disease scrofula could be cured if you were touched by a king or queen. It's a disease that often went away on its own, giving the impression that the magical monarch was taking care of it. This healing power was said to prove their God-given right to rule.

Doctors at the time didn't understand what was causing the disease and were helpless to treat it. Some thought it was caused by corrupt air, while others believed it was God's punishment for sinners.

Cures included drinking rotten treacle, bathing in wee, sitting in a sewer and strapping a live chicken to the head. People even whipped themselves in the streets in the hope that God would see they'd already had enough punishment, and decide to spare them.

CHRIS: But couldn't this backfire? What if God thought you enjoyed punishment and wanted more?

Another famous plague outbreak happened in 1665. This was a mixture of two utterly horrible types: bubonic plague spread by rat fleas and pneumonic plague spread by sneezes. Crazy cures this time included jumping over lavender, putting a gold coin in the mouth, and leeches. Good old leeches, eh? If in doubt, get the leech jar out.

As if the plague wasn't horrific enough, everyone had to put up with the sight of doctors dressed as nightmarish birds. This is because they wore special costumes to protect themselves. It consisted of a beak-like mask, a gown, leather gloves and a hat. The beak was filled with lavender to protect them from the bad air. Even if they saved plague victims, they'd probably have made everyone else die of fright.

Some think the plague was wiped out by the Great Fire of London the following year, but it actually died out in the winter of 1665. You've got to feel sorry for those Londoners, though. One year they get the plague, the next they get a fire. They must have been wondering what 1667 would have in store. Tiger infestation? Flesh-eating spiders? Dragon attack?

XAND: Our examination of the skin leads us to one of the most important chapters in medical history.

CHRIS: If you found yourself covered in pus-filled blisters in the eighteenth century, you'd have been very worried indeed.

XAND: This was a sign of smallpox, which killed millions every year.

CHRIS: But then a man called Edward Jenner made a discovery that would eventually wipe the horrid disease off the face of the earth.

The nasty disease of smallpox blighted mankind for thousands of years. The only prevention that worked was deliberately giving someone the disease with infected scabs when they were young, which meant they'd be immune from a more serious version later on. But this was still very dangerous.

Edward Jenner was an English doctor who'd suffered this treatment as a child. His arm had been cut open, smallpox scabs had been shoved in and the cut bandaged up again. As well as being even more disgusting than eating someone else's bogies, this made the young Jenner very ill. No wonder he was keen to find an alternative treatment.

Jenner had heard that milkmaids never caught smallpox, and wondered if it was because of cowpox, which caused blisters on their hands after they milked infected cows. Using the eight-year-old son of his gardener as a guinea pig, Jenner performed one of the most important (and gross) experiments in medical history.

Jenner injected the boy, who was called James Phipps, with pus from a milkmaid's hand, giving him cowpox. The poor boy might have thought he'd done enough for science at that point, but he was wrong. Next, Jenner injected him with rancid pus from a smallpox victim. If Jenner's theory had been wrong, the boy could have suffered a feverish, messy death. But he was fine.

The experiment showed that cowpox could be used as a vaccination against the much more serious disease of smallpox. Since then, vaccination programmes have been used throughout the world, with millions of people being injected with mild viruses to stop them getting more serious ones.

Smallpox was completely eradicated by 1979. So, three cheers to Edward Jenner for discovering how to get rid of the nasty disease; and *four* cheers for James Phipps for doing the hard part.

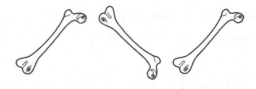

GROSS OUT

If you applied for the job of 'gong farmer' in Tudor England expecting pleasant agricultural work, you'd have been in for a shock. A gong farmer was someone who dug poo out of cesspits and carried it away, outside the town walls. The pay was good but the risks were high: many gong farmers got seriously ill from all the poo fumes.

Heroes of Medicine:
Alexander Fleming (and Howard Florey and Ernst Chain)

Scottish scientist Alexander Fleming discovered the miracle drug penicillin in 1929 when some fungus mould accidentally fell on to his Petri dish. Penicillin has saved millions of lives since, making this one of the most fortunate accidents in human history.

But what many don't know is that Alexander Fleming didn't fully understand what he'd discovered, and it wasn't until a decade later that two other scientists, Howard Florey and Ernst Chain, picked up his research and realised penicillin could be a wonder drug.

So that was another ten years of pain patients had to suffer while the miracle mould sat on a lab shelf, waiting for someone to realise how awesome it was! Still, better late than never, and penicillin helped to save the lives of thousands of Allied soldiers in World War Two.

All three men were given the Nobel Prize in 1945, though most people only remember Alexander Fleming now.

QUIZ

Which Greek god do doctors swear by when taking the Hippocratic Oath?

A. Apollo, god of the sun
B. Hades, god of the underworld
C. Darren, god of tidy waiting rooms

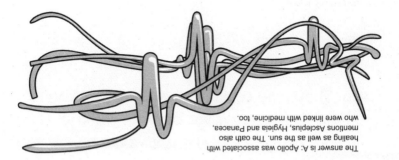

The answer is A: Apollo was associated with healing as well as the sun. The oath also mentions Asclepius, Hygieia and Panacea, who were linked with medicine, too.

BODY TRICKS:
Through the Floor

CHRIS: This amazing body trick will make your friends think their feet are sinking through the floor.

XAND: Get a friend to lie down with their eyes closed, then take hold of their feet and lift them up for a minute or two.

CHRIS: You might want to hold your breath before starting the trick if your friend has stinky feet.

XAND: The trick will be worth the blast of foot pong, we promise you.

CHRIS: Then lower their feet down to the floor, very slowly.

XAND: Your friend will think their feet are back on floor level ages before they really are.

CHRIS: They'll be convinced you've dug a hole in the floor, even if you perform the trick in your living room, where it would be impossible to do this without causing loads of damage.

XAND: The reason for this is that when you hold your friend's legs up, the nerves in their joints relax and stop telling their brains where their legs are.

CHRIS: Unable to see anything, their confused brain will keep trying to work out the position of their legs, and keep getting it wrong.

XAND: It's a trick that will take their breath away.

CHRIS: Even if you have to hold yours while you're doing it.

THE HAIR

XAND: Hair has fascinated us throughout history.

CHRIS: Some bizarre styles in how it's worn have come and gone throughout the ages, from the side-locks of Ancient Egypt, and medieval braids, to your dad in his wedding photo.

XAND: But the problems start when the stuff begins to fall out.

CHRIS: Self-conscious men have long called on doctors to cure their baldness. And some of the cures have been very strange indeed.

Roman author Pliny the Elder believed rubbing mouse droppings on a bald head would make hair grow back. He was wrong, though perhaps a pile of mouse poo could pass for a full head of hair from a distance. As long as you don't mind reeking of mouse poo, of course.

Another famous Roman had a much better way of curing baldness. Julius Caesar grew the hair on the back of his head long, swept it to the front and fixed it in place with a laurel wreath. It was a completely foolproof method, except for when there was a light breeze. This 'comb-over' style enjoyed a revival in the twentieth century, when hairspray was invented. But even the strongest spray can't stop the comb-over from unravelling in a high wind. It's a risky strategy, and quite a lot of effort to avoid being called 'slaphead'.

The twentieth century brought many bizarre baldness cures, such as 'thermocaps'. These were strange, dome-shaped hats that heated the top of your head. They didn't work, but they did make you look like a weird alien while you were using them, which was quite cool.

Shortly afterwards, vacuum pumps were invented that were meant to increase blood circulation and restore lost hair.

XAND: People could probably have used them as hoovers when they found they didn't work.

This 'brilliant' invention was soon followed by hair transplants. These graft hair follicles from one part of the body to another to revive bald patches. Unlike the other treatments, they actually work, and are still used today. They're more effort than simply slapping a wig on your head, though.

Better news was to come for baldies in the twenty-first century. Shaved heads became fashionable, and even men with working follicles chose to be hairless. Bald men could at last cast aside their mouse poo and thermocaps and display their shiny domes to the world.

XAND: At least baldies don't run the risk of head lice.

CHRIS: These wingless parasites have clung on to our scalps for centuries, treating themselves to blood and making us itch.

 113

XAND: We've been trying to get rid of them for centuries, too, but the cheeky little freeloaders have clung on.

In Ancient Greece, garlic and oregano was recommended for head lice, which sounds more like a delicious pizza topping than a medicine. In Ancient Rome, Pliny the Elder recommended rubbing the scalp with dog fat.

CHRIS: But was it worth sacrificing the family dog just to get rid of lice? It was surely better to put up with them than make poor Fido pay the price.

Mustard, salt and vinegar were all recommended for lice in the Middle Ages – basically, pour some condiments on your head. They'd probably have used tomato sauce too, if it had been invented.

In the twentieth century, the US army regularly doused people with insect powder to kill their lice, but the practice was stopped when the powder was found to be dangerous to humans, too.

DID YOU KNOW?

A German doctor named Johann Christian Reil thought of a cruel and bonkers way to treat patients who had trouble paying attention – he invented a piano made of cats. A row of cats would be placed in a line and their tails would be struck each time a key was pressed, making them screech out a melody. The idea was that the patient would be unable to ignore this bizarre spectacle, and their attention problems would be solved. But the problems would just be beginning for the poor moggies . . .

Unlike many blights from the past, head lice are still with us, sneaking around our hair and quaffing our blood. We now treat them with medicated lotions and sprays, and wet combing, which involves washing the hair and going through it with a fine-toothed comb. Let's hope we find a way to wipe them out for good soon.

XAND: Pop down to the hairdressers these days and you might get a blast of hairspray and a friendly chat about your holiday.

CHRIS: What you won't get is surgery.

XAND: Yet that's exactly what people in the Middle Ages could expect.

Doctors in the Middle Ages didn't like to actually touch patients, so where could you go if you needed some actual surgery? Surprisingly, it was barbers who filled that gap in the market. At the same time as getting the latest fashionable medieval haircut, you could get a rotten tooth pulled, a

boil lanced and have a couple of leeches fitted. In fact, if you asked the barber to 'Take a bit off the sides' in the Middle Ages, you'd have to make it very clear you didn't want your arms amputated.

Heroes of Medicine:
Ignaz Semmelweis

In 1846, an Austrian hospital worker made a shocking suggestion that outraged the medical establishment. He said doctors should wash their hands.

Semmelweis had noted the large number of women who were dying during childbirth at Vienna General Hospital. Many of them were found to be filled with a smelly kind of 'milk' when they were dissected. We now know that this wasn't milk at all, but pus from infection. Ewww!

Semmelweis compared two maternity wards within the clinic, as one of them was suffering a lot more deaths than the other. He realised that the doctors who worked in the less fortunate clinic also handled dead bodies, and thought this might be the reason. He suggested the doctors wash their hands between touching the corpses and delivering the babies.

The plan worked and the number of childbirth deaths fell, but many doctors were outraged by the suggestion that they'd been partly responsible for the deaths of the mothers.

QUIZ

Where and when were the first three blood groups discovered?

A. Transylvania in 1897
B. Vienna in 1900
C. New York in 1903

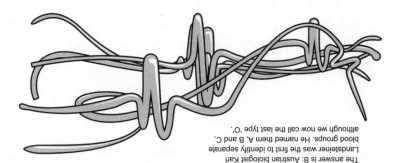

The answer is B: Austrian biologist Karl Landsteiner was the first to identify separate blood groups. He named them A, B and C, although we now call the last type 'O'.

BODY TRICKS:
Magnetic Fingers

CHRIS: Here's a trick that will make your friends lose control of their fingers.

XAND: Get them to clench their fists and spin their arms around as fast as they can.

CHRIS: After they've been doing it for a while, get them to hold their hands parallel, but not quite touching.

XAND: While they're doing this, pretend you're using magic powers to move their fingers together.

CHRIS: They'll find that no matter how hard they try and keep their fingers apart, they'll curl towards each other.

XAND: That's because they'll have clenched their fists into tight balls while they were spinning their arms around.

CHRIS: The muscles in their fingers get used to contracting, and want to keep on squeezing.

XAND: Which means they'll have to go through life with their fingers stuck together until you agree to turn your magic powers off.

CHRIS: Er . . . no, it doesn't. Their fingers will soon go back to normal on their own.

CHRIS: Come in, take a seat.

XAND: Visit your local GP today and you'll get a friendly welcome like this.

CHRIS: What seems to be the problem?

XAND: But just a few hundred years ago, your doctor would have stabbed you.

CHRIS: Hmmm . . . I see. And when do you feel these pains?

 127

XAND: Because for centuries, bloodletting was regarded as one of the best cures for a huge range of diseases.

Hippocrates in Ancient Greece and Galen in Ancient Rome both believed the body contained four types of fluid known as 'humours': blood, phlegm, black bile and yellow bile. They thought that a person was healthy when all these humours were in balance, but got ill when they had too much or too little of one.

Curing excess blood was easy: all the doctor had to do was whip out a scalpel and start cutting away.

Countless illnesses were blamed on excess blood. Galen thought headaches and fevers were caused by it and recommended chopping into a patient's vein and letting it 'breathe'.

CHRIS: By which he meant letting blood spurt around the place, as in a horror film.

The earliest bloodletting was done with sharpened stones, but a series of gruesome instruments were developed to help doctors slash. There was a

 128

lancet, which was a double-edged blade with an ebony or ivory handle, while a spring lancet featured a blade that could be released by a button. And the aptly named 'scarificator' featured a row of spring-loaded blades that could make several cuts at once.

An American doctor called Joseph Snodgrass loved his spring lancet so much he wrote a poem about it:

> I love thee, bloodstained, faithful friend!
> As warrior loves his sword or shield
> For how on thee did I depend
> When foes of life were in the field!

Bloodletting wasn't only gory and misguided: it was dangerous. Blood is vital to our survival and losing too much can be harmful. History is full of accounts of bloodletting that now make painful reading. One example is George Washington, the first president of the United States of America, who was bedridden with a throat infection in 1799. He demanded his doctors bleed him to cure it. Over five pints of blood were drained from him in the ten hours before he died – just under half the amount of blood he had at all!

 129

DID YOU KNOW?

We now know blood contains both red and white cells, as well as platelets. But when white blood cells were first spotted through a microscope in the eighteenth century, they were thought to be bits of pus.

CHRIS: Amazingly, spring lancets and scarificators weren't the most horrific thing used to drain blood.

XAND: For centuries, doctors brought along some slimy little pals to help them out.

CHRIS: Hospital middle management?

XAND: No. They were leeches, and they were used as a treatment for almost everything.

Leeches are a type of worm with 125 teeth, and who love to suck blood. They were widely used in medicine from the ancient world right up until the nineteenth century.

As with bloodletting, they were used to drain excess blood and restore the balance of the body. Leeches were applied to all parts of the body, including throats and bottoms.

The demand was so great that the creatures were sometimes farmed for medical use, but spare a thought for the poor unfortunates who took jobs as leech collectors. One of the ways they harvested them was to wade into filthy swamps and let the little bloodsuckers latch on to their legs. Then they could pull them off and sell them to doctors. Patience was important, however: yank the creature away too soon and they'd wound themselves AND make the creature unsellable.

Leeches fell out of favour towards the end of the nineteenth century, but they've made a surprising comeback in recent years. It's been found that their saliva contains a chemical that stops blood from clotting, which can help with things like skin grafts. While there's no doubt that, over the ages, doctors went over the top with their use of the slimy little suckers, it seems they weren't so crazy to use them in medicine after all.

XAND: Except for the bit about sticking them on bottoms. That was crazy.

CHRIS: Believe it or not, some people used to think they could make themselves better by drinking blood.

XAND: They were known as 'vampires'. They used to live in coffins and . . .

CHRIS: No, these are actual humans we're talking about here.

XAND: Really? Are you sure they didn't have capes and fangs? You know how these vampires like to trick everyone.

The fifteenth-century Italian writer Marsilio Ficino believed the elderly should drink the blood of the young – which could make a trip to see your grandparents rather awkward. He suggested that when the moon was waxing, old people should cut open the veins of a youth and drink an ounce of blood, followed by the same amount of syrup or wine. Luckily, his claim was based on hard, scientific evidence: he said that witches did it, so humans should too.

In Ancient Rome, it was believed the blood of gladiators was good for curing things, and it was thought to be especially good at treating epilepsy. The superstition that blood could help with epilepsy lasted so long that the famous author of fairy tales, Hans Christian Andersen, mentioned it in the nine-teenth century, when he claimed to have seen an epileptic drinking the blood of an executed prisoner.

Blood wasn't the only part of a dead body that was considered healthy to consume. The seventeenth-century English doctor, Sir Thomas Willis, made a drink that consisted of ground human skull and chocolate. Yum to the chocolate part, yuck to the human skull part.

Disgusting though it might seem, dried corpse – known as 'mumie' – was commonly taken as medicine just a few hundred years ago. Even King Charles II used to drink a mixture of alcohol and human skull. Next time you spot him on a wall chart of kings and queens, remember that he was a cannibal. Eeek!

XAND: Dead bodies weren't just used to provide a bedtime snack for the king, however. Doctors needed them for examination.

 135

CHRIS: To understand the workings of organs like the heart, doctors needed corpses to dissect.

XAND: But getting your hands on a fresh corpse wasn't easy.

CHRIS: This problem lead to one of the grimmest periods in medical history.

XAND: It's a horrid tale of grave robbing under the cloak of night, and foul murder, so only read on if you dare . . .

In the early nineteenth century, doctors were only allowed to dissect the corpses of executed murderers. At hangings, fights broke out between the families of the dead and people who wanted to sell the corpses to surgeons.

CHRIS: And thereby ruining the innocent entertainment of the massive crowds who'd turned out to watch the hanging. The selfishness of some people, eh?

The demand for bodies was met by the work of body-snatchers or 'resurrection men', who would steal corpses from their graves at night. It must have been one of the grossest jobs in history. Bodysnatchers became such a problem that relatives often had to keep watch over the graves of their loved ones to make sure they weren't pinched, while some cemeteries even put iron bars over graves until the corpses were too rotten to be of use to surgeons.

The situation got even more grisly in Scotland, where William Burke and William Hare found an easy solution to the problem of supplying bodies to Dr Robert Knox: they simply created the corpses themselves by murdering people. They bumped off sixteen unfortunate victims before being caught.

Burke was hanged in front of a huge crowd, and was eventually dissected in front of medical students.

XAND: It's what he would have wanted.

This event proved so popular that there wasn't enough room in the anatomy theatre and students had to file past his corpse in batches.

New laws were soon passed that allowed more corpses to be supplied to medical schools, and the dead could, once again, rest peacefully in their graves. But while Burke and Hare may be gone, their grim story lives on in history books, horror films and even a children's skipping rhyme:

> Up the close and down the stair
> But and ben wi' Burke and Hare.
> Burke's the butcher, Hare's the thief
> Knox the boy that buys the beef.

CHRIS: Not all breakthroughs came at such a grisly price.

XAND: But some did come from some very odd situations.

CHRIS: One of the most famous medical instruments ever was invented because a patient was a little on the, er . . . large side.

In 1816 French doctor René Laennec wanted to examine an obese woman with a heart problem. Her weight was making it difficult for him to listen to her heart in the usual way: being a typical nineteenth-century gentleman, Laennec was embarrassed about the need for plunging his ear into her body to listen to her heart and lungs. So he used a rolled-up piece of paper instead.

Laennec had created the first ever stethoscope, an instrument that magnifies the sounds of the heart and chest and allows doctors to diagnose illness. We still use it today and it's helped millions of doctors catch serious chest problems early. If only the overweight patient had known the effect she would have.

Heroes of Medicine: Louis Pasteur

If you've ever had pasteurised milk, French scientist Louis Pasteur is the man to thank. In fact, you should thank him even if you have no idea what pasteurised milk is, because his germ theory of disease changed the world for ever.

Pasteur wasn't the first person to research into bacteria – the tiny life forms that release poisons

HEY! WHAT ARE YOU LOOKING AT?

inside our bodies and make us feel ill, but he was the first to realise they attack the body from outside and cause disease. Before him, everyone thought it was the other way round – that diseases caused bacteria.

His brilliant brainwave helped us understand diseases such as anthrax, cholera and tuberculosis, and prevent them through vaccination. A spin-off of his work was pasteurised milk, which is heated to kill the bacteria it contains so it doesn't go sour.

So if you've ever poured pasteurised milk on your cereal, you can thank Monsieur Pasteur that it doesn't taste like cheese. And also be glad that you don't have anthrax, cholera or tuberculosis. You probably wouldn't feel like eating any cereal at all if you did.

QUIZ

In which year was the first artificial heart implanted?

A. In 360 BC by Hippocrates
B. In 1854 by Florence Nightingale
C. In 1969 by Denton Cooley

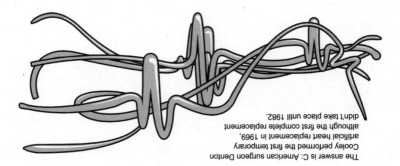

The answer is C: American surgeon Denton Cooley performed the first temporary artificial heart replacement in 1969, although the first complete replacement didn't take place until 1982.

CHRIS: If you're reading this, you're probably breathing.

XAND: If not, you're either seriously ill or dead, and should seek help.

CHRIS: If you are breathing, thank your lungs.

XAND: You'd certainly notice if they stopped working. Many horrible illnesses from history have affected the lungs.

The mid-twentieth century brought a wave of the disease polio, which made it difficult for people to breathe. A machine called an 'iron lung' was created to help. It was a huge steel chamber

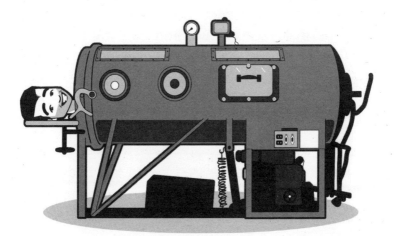

that you'd lie inside with your head poking out. Pumps controlled the air pressure inside, making you breathe in and out. Photos showing rows of children with their heads sticking out of huge steel drums look very strange, but the contraption helped to save thousands of lives.

Another deadly disease that affects the lungs is tuberculosis. The ancient Greek writer Hippocrates said it was so deadly that he recommended doctors avoid treating it: the patient would only die anyway, and then everyone would think you were a bad doctor.

The Romans at least had a go at stopping it. Some of them believed it was caused by winds blowing from north to north west, and that the best way to prevent it was to build more walls. Of course, it wouldn't have worked, but at least they'd have been helping the local building trade.

Some in the Middle Ages believed the disease was caused by demons trapped inside the body. This seems silly to us now, but it must have been pretty frightening to see a victim, back in the days before the lungs were fully understood, coughing up blood.

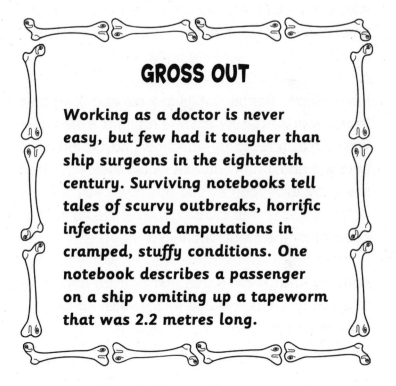

GROSS OUT

Working as a doctor is never easy, but few had it tougher than ship surgeons in the eighteenth century. Surviving notebooks tell tales of scurvy outbreaks, horrific infections and amputations in cramped, stuffy conditions. One notebook describes a passenger on a ship vomiting up a tapeworm that was 2.2 metres long.

By the nineteenth century, the disease was killing millions every year. Many treatments were attempted, including a gruesome one known as 'plombage'. This involved shoving acrylic balls into someone's lungs so they'd collapse and then heal again. Luckily, the disease is now treated with medicine rather than ping pong balls.

Yet another horrific disease that had a horrific treatment was pneumonia. This is a swelling in your lungs caused by infection and, in the days before it could be controlled with medicine, lungs would be swamped by vile pus. One way doctors coped with this was to remove an entire rib so they could drain the lung. Ouch!

XAND: The lungs were also the focus of one of the most controversial periods in medical history.

CHRIS: It all started when medical researchers worked out that smoking can lead to lung cancer.

XAND: It's not controversial any more, of course, but it was for a surprisingly long time.

Tobacco was thought to be good for you when it was introduced to Europe in the sixteenth century. There was a dramatic rise in lung cancer in the early twentieth century when smoking became affordable for everyone, but no one could work out what was causing it. Some thought it was air pollution, while others thought it was because of the sorts of jobs people did.

Some researchers thought cigarettes were to blame, but it took a long time for them to convince everyone else. A lot of smokers didn't want to admit their addiction was harmful, and cigarette companies didn't want to lose money. Some of them even ran adverts featuring doctors recommending certain types of cigarette for health benefits, which look incredibly bizarre now.

Eventually, the evidence became too strong, and cigarette companies were forced to slap warnings on their packets. It was also found that cigarette smoke could endanger other people too, which led to a ban on smoking in many public places.

DID YOU KNOW?

Many famous products were originally marketed for their health benefits. For example, some fizzy soft drinks were said to cure headaches and help with digestion. The claims turned out to be untrue, but the drinks caught on and are still with us today.

 152

Heroes of Medicine:
Hieronymus Fabricus

Hieronymus Fabricus was an Italian surgeon who lived in the sixteenth century. His dissections helped us understand the human body, but the most interesting thing about them was their popularity with the public.

Dissections were an acceptable form of entertainment in the sixteenth century – some records even mention musical accompaniments. After all, what could make for a better day out than a lovely tune and a sliced corpse?

Hieronymus Fabricus was like the Justin Bieber of the public dissection world, and his shows were so difficult to get into that he had to build a bigger theatre to fit all his fans inside. Body parts were passed around the audience, but stealing them to take home and show your friends was strictly forbidden.

Many people were outraged when the German anatomist Gunther Von Hagens began staging public autopsies a few years ago, but he was actually reviving a centuries-old tradition.

QUIZ

How many doctors and nurses left the UK to help soldiers on the front line during the First World War?

A. 1,800 – enough to fill one modern hospital

B. 18,000 – enough to fill ten modern hospitals

C. 118,000 – enough to fill one hundred modern hospitals

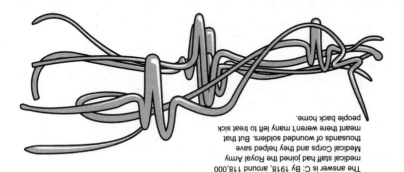

The answer is C: By 1918, around 118,000 medical staff had joined the Royal Army Medical Corps and they helped save thousands of wounded soldiers. But that meant there weren't many left to treat sick people back home.

THE LIMBS

XAND: Your arms and legs are very useful if you want to pick something up or run for the bus.

CHRIS: But, unlike other bits of your body such as your head, they're not essential and you could live without them.

XAND: Throughout history, people have overcome the loss of limbs with prosthetics.

There are many mentions of prosthetic limbs in early writing. The Roman historian Herodotus tells the story of a prisoner who cut off his own foot to escape chains and replaced it with a wooden one. Pliny the Elder describes a soldier who lost his arm and replaced it with an iron one that could hold a shield.

Limbs were often substituted with simple things like peg legs in the Middle Ages. They live on today as part of pirate fancy-dress costumes, along with eye patches, shoulder-mounted parrots and pirate accents.

In the sixteenth century the French surgeon Ambroise Paré developed more sophisticated prosthetics that resembled real limbs. He even

designed a leg that could bend at the knee and lock when standing up, and a mechanical hand full of springs and pulleys.

The large number of soldiers who lost their limbs in the First World War created an unprecedented demand for prosthetics. An entire hospital was set up in London to produce and fit wooden legs.

Over the last hundred years, artificial limb technology has developed at an astounding rate. Light and sophisticated limbs made from plastic and carbon fibre have replaced the peg legs and hook hands of the past.

CHRIS: Another problem seen during the First World War was called 'trench foot'.

XAND: It happened when soldiers' feet were soaked for days in cold, wet trenches.

CHRIS: Their feet went even smellier and more disgusting than yours when you forget to change your socks.

When your body gets too cold, your brain has to make a decision about which parts it needs the most, and warm blood is diverted to your vital internal organs. This can be bad news for feet, which don't then get enough blood, and so start to go soft and wrinkly.

The flesh on the foot dies, making it easy prey for germs and bacteria. Trench foot was very stinky, very painful and sometimes entire feet had to be lopped off.

DID YOU KNOW?

When the eighth president of Mexico had his leg amputated in 1838, he had it buried with full military honours. He replaced it with a cork leg, but this was captured by US troops in the Mexican–American War.

To prevent it, regular foot inspections had to be carried out in the trenches. A gross and gruesome job, but one that helped save the feet of millions of soldiers.

XAND: Modern surgeons have to work under intense pressure to perform life-saving operations.

CHRIS: But just a couple of centuries ago, doctors were so concerned about speed they learned to perform operations in mere seconds.

XAND: Unsurprisingly, this obsession with speed sometimes had ouch-tastic consequences.

THE LIMBS

Robert Liston was a Scottish surgeon who worked in the early nineteenth century. He was known for his amazing speed and it's thought he could amputate a leg in just a couple of minutes. He encouraged onlookers to time him on their pocket watches as he sliced away with his scalpel while his assistants held the terrified patients down.

Liston had good reason to be quick, as he was working in the years before anaesthetic. He'd cut through the flesh, saw through bone and tie arteries and blood vessels at lightning speed. A box full of sawdust would be waiting to receive the severed limb.

His patients could be grateful their ordeal was over so quickly, unless there was an accident along the way – according to a book about Liston, he once sliced through the fingers of his assistant and into the body of a spectator while amputating a leg. The patient, assistant and onlooker all died, which must make it one of the least successful operations of all time.

Heroes of Medicine: Owen Thomas

At the start of the First World War, eight out of ten soldiers who broke their legs died. By the end, the figure had fallen to just one in ten. It was all down to Owen Thomas, who invented a type of splint we still use today.

His traction splint works by pulling the muscles back and allowing the bones to be realigned. It fixes broken bones, controls blood loss and helps keep infection out.

The 'Thomas splint' is still used in modern emergency departments. If you ever have the misfortune to find yourself in one, at least be grateful you're in a clean hospital and not a muddy trench with bullets whizzing around you.

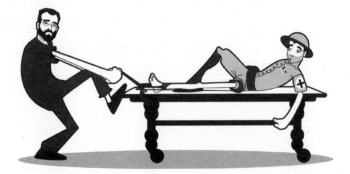

GROSS OUT

A doctor in the middle of the nineteenth century came up with an interesting cure for tapeworms. He suggested tying a piece of cheese to some string and lowering it into a patient's stomach. When the greedy tapeworm started to scoff the cheese, the doctor would yank the string and the patient would be free of the parasite. Sadly, he was overestimating the tapeworm: the simple creature can't smell or see, and would have no way of knowing there was a savoury treat up for grabs.

CHRIS: We've all suffered from bellyache after eating too much . . .

XAND: Or eating the wrong things . . .

CHRIS: Or eating too quickly . . .

XAND: Or eating too many of the wrong things too quickly.

CHRIS: And so has everyone else in history. Stomach treatments have always been in demand.

Ancient Egyptians drank a mixture of herbs, milk and animal fats while reciting a spell asking the gods to rid them of the evil spirits in their stomachs.

XAND: Going to see the doctor back then must have been like visiting Hogwarts.

Roman writer Galen believed half-cooked eggs could help with stomach problems, as he reckoned eggs had life-giving properties because chickens hatched from them. Although half-cooked eggs could cause stomach problems rather than cure them.

In the Middle Ages, a drink made from daffodil bulbs was given to people suffering from stomach pain, but it wasn't meant to soothe their pain – it was meant to make them spew up whatever was causing the problem. Better to give daffodil bulb juice a miss, then.

CHRIS: If you've ever had a croaky voice, you might have been told that you had a frog in your throat.

XAND: But it was frogs in your stomach you had to be worried about a few hundred years ago . . .

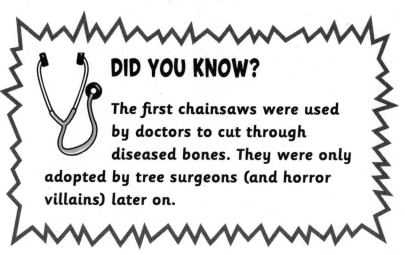

DID YOU KNOW?

The first chainsaws were used by doctors to cut through diseased bones. They were only adopted by tree surgeons (and horror villains) later on.

For ages, stomach problems were blamed on frogs and snakes that lived inside the belly; some medical books from the seventeenth and eighteenth centuries even describe cases of painful frog and toad infections.

In one, frogspawn in the stomach lining was said to have caused the creatures to breed; in another, a patient was said to have vomited an entire colony of frogs on to the floor. Either the serious problem of stomach frogs has been wiped out since, or the doctors in question were talking complete rubbish.

CHRIS: Stick too many crisps, pizzas and sweets in your stomach and you'll get overweight.

XAND: While fuller figures were once fashionable, our recent obsession with thinness has led to some very weird weight-loss fads.

The pressure to be thin in the twentieth century created a craze for dieting on which all sorts of odd people tried to cash in. An American called Horace Fletcher thought that if you chewed your food hundreds of times before swallowing it, you'd put less weight on AND get more vitamins from it. He reckoned that if you used his system you'd only need to poo once a fortnight and it would smell no worse than a 'hot biscuit'. (Try not to think about *that* next time you're eating a hot biscuit.) But, to be fair, if you had to chew something hundreds of times, it would take all the joy out of eating, so perhaps you'd want less of it.

In the 1920s a product called 'La Mar Reducing Soap' claimed to be able to 'wash away fat and years of age'. It was one of several weight-loss soaps marketed by conmen around this time. You could eat as much as you liked and wash it all away in a nice, relaxing bath. Complete nonsense, of course, but maybe it's just as well. Anyone who stayed in the bath too long might have risked coming out looking like a skinny new-born baby.

The grossest diet of all time was surely the tapeworm diet. A tapeworm is a slimy creature that lives inside you, absorbing your food and laying eggs. They can cause weight loss, as well as diarrhoea and vomiting.

CHRIS: How lovely and slim they must have looked, ridden with parasites and spewing all over the place.

If you ever need to lose weight, eating healthily and exercising regularly are the key. Deliberately giving yourself worms is not.

XAND: As well as suffering many painful ailments, the stomach also produced one of the weirdest medicines ever.

CHRIS: A 'bezoar' is a solid clump of indigestible material found in the stomach or digestive tract.

XAND: Instead of throwing these disgusting things away, people prized them, convinced they had magical healing powers. Bezoars were also thought to protect people against being poisoned, so some people popped them into their drinks before sipping them. It might not have worked, but at least it added a delicious note of stomach lining to your favourite beverage.

In 1603 a man tried to sue someone who'd sold him a faulty bezoar for a hundred pounds. The judge ruled that he had no right to get his money back, but stopped short of sending him to prison for gullibility.

One of the weirdest types of bezoar is the 'trichobezoar', which is made by eating hair. These can sometimes be huge, stretching from the stomach to the bowels, and might have to be removed by surgery. In animals, these are known as 'hairballs', and you might have seen your cat cough one up on to the carpet.

Just to be clear, they have no medical value whatsoever. If you see Tiddles retching one up, DO NOT put it in the medicine cabinet. Your family won't thank you.

CHRIS: The knowledge we have about the stomach is all thanks to early pioneers of medicine.

XAND: Some of whom went beyond the call of duty to help us understand digestion.

CHRIS: One of them even drank his own puke . . .

In the late eighteenth century, the Italian scientist

Lazzaro Spallanzani conducted a series of gross experiments into human digestion. He made himself sick and examined the spew to see the effects of gastric juices. He even swallowed bits of food on long pieces of string so he could pull them up again, for examination. And he also drank his own vomit and then puked it up *again*. A true example of someone who really suffered for science. Unless he just had really weird taste in food, of course.

DID YOU KNOW?

Nostalgia was classified as a disease until the end of the nineteenth century. It was first identified by the Swiss doctor Johannes Hofer in 1688 as an extreme homesickness that caused fainting, fever and stomach pain. Maybe one day you'll remember reading this book so fondly it will make you faint.

Heroes of Medicine: Alexis St. Martin

Over the course of eleven years in the early nineteenth century, Dr William Beaumont performed a series of experiments that changed our understanding of the human stomach for ever. But the real hero was his patient, Alexis St. Martin.

A bullet had left a permanent hole in St. Martin's stomach, allowing Dr Beaumont to examine it. Alexis ate raw meat and let the doctor pull it out through the hole to see how it had changed. He let him poke a thermometer into the hole, and he even let him drink a cup of his stomach juice. Eww!

Dr Beaumont's experiments paved the way for modern stomach treatments, but it's his long-suffering patient we should really thank.

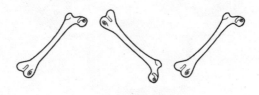

QUIZ

Which horrible disease killed up to 200 million people in Europe in the middle of the fourteenth century?

A. The Black Death
B. The Yellow Fever
C. The Purple Peril

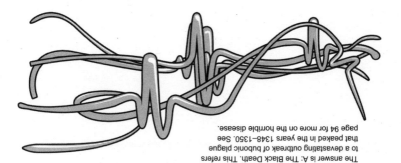

The answer is A: The Black Death. This refers to a devastating outbreak of bubonic plague that peaked in the years 1348–1350. See page 94 for more on the horrible disease.

THE BLADDER

CHRIS: Imagine if your body produced an endless supply of golden medicine that could be used to treat a wide variety of illnesses.

XAND: Now imagine if all you had to do to get it was go to the toilet and relax.

CHRIS: We're talking, of course, about wee.

XAND: Sadly, wee isn't a miracle cure for anything, but that hasn't stopped people throughout history believing the opposite.

Many cultures have believed that drinking wee is good for you. The Roman writer Cato thought ill people should taste the urine of people who ate a lot of cabbage. He was so convinced the wee of a cabbage-eater was good for the health, he believed babies who were washed in it would never become ill.

The Romans thought wee had all sorts of uses. They even used it to whiten their teeth. That might sound crazy, but urine contains ammonia, which can be used to clean things, so maybe they were on to something. You're still better off with toothpaste, though.

Believe it or not, some people are STILL convinced that drinking wee is good for them. This is known as 'urine therapy'.

CHRIS: You should be careful if you ever visit the house of someone who swears by it. Especially if the glass of lemonade they've just handed you is suspiciously warm.

XAND: Just to confirm, drinking wee and bathing in it do NOT have any medical benefits.

CHRIS: Unless you count smelling like the inside of a phone box as a benefit.

XAND: Sorry to break it to you, but wee has pretty much no use at all.

CHRIS: It can't even help with jellyfish stings or athlete's foot, despite what people might have told you.

Sometimes folk remedies survive as myths years after they've been shown to be useless. An example is the use of wee to cure jellyfish stings.

Jellyfish venom can be incredibly painful. It burns the skin and causes it to itch, and scratching only makes things worse. So, would getting a friend to relieve themselves on you relieve your pain, too? Sadly, no. In fact, it could make it worse. And it will certainly cause embarrassment. Vinegar could help, so they'd be much better off finding the nearest fish and chip shop than weeing on you.

These days, it's so easy to find out about genuine treatments, it's strange that anyone still believes in these sorts of folk cures. It just goes to show the power of advice passed on by word of mouth.

CHRIS: As well as being touted as an unlikely miracle cure, urine has also been used as a way of checking health.

XAND: Urine tests are still used today for things like pregnancy, diabetes and whether you've been eating asparagus or not.

CHRIS: But there was a time when wee was thought to reveal everything.

The Ancient Greeks checked wee to see if someone's blood, phlegm, yellow bile and black bile were in balance. The Romans took the obsession even further, believing you could tell someone's future from examining their wee.

XAND: Did no one back then have a sense of smell?

Doctors in the Middle Ages were so fascinated with wee they gathered it in special flasks decorated with jewels. Many doctors in those days were forbidden from touching patients, so it's perhaps not surprising that they got so obsessed with it.

CHRIS: But storing it in a bejewelled flask seems a little over the top.

A doctor called Isaac Judaeus created a chart that could tell what illness someone had from the colour of their wee. Although he was wrong about most of it, you *can* tell some things from the colour of your wee. For example, if it's almost clear, it means you've been drinking enough water; if it's almost orange, it means you haven't been drinking enough. Watch out for orange wee in the summer, and make sure you've had enough liquids.

Some weird doctors even went as far as tasting wee in the name of scientific progress. A seventeenth-century English doctor called Thomas Willis observed the link between sweet-tasting urine and diabetes. Valuable research, but a high price to pay. Couldn't he have got his assistant to do it for him?

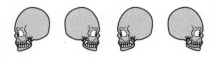

Heroes of Medicine:
Henri Dunant and the Red Cross

The International Committee of the Red Cross was founded by a Swiss businessman called Henri Dunant in 1863. He was appalled by the suffering

of soldiers he saw on a battlefield, and created an organisation to help those wounded in war.

Hundreds of Red Cross nurses came to the aid of soldiers in the First World War. Hospitals were set up in schools and town halls to treat the unprecedented number of casualties, and thousands of people volunteered to help.

Many private houses had to be converted into hospitals during the Second World War, as tens of thousands of soldiers and civilians needed help. Once again, the nurses were helped out by huge numbers of Red Cross volunteers.

The good work of the Red Cross continues today. It's sad that war hasn't gone away over the past century and a half, but at least these true heroes and heroines of medicine have been there to help.

QUIZ

What did James Watson and Francis Crick discover in 1953 that has been dubbed 'the building blocks of life'?

A. DNA
B. Minecraft
C. Lego

The answer is A: they discovered DNA, tiny strands inside your body that are shaped like twisty ladders and determine everything about you, from the size of your nose to the curliness of your hair. Thanks, twisty ladders!

CHRIS: Sadly, our tour through medical history is coming to an end.

XAND: And we've chosen to end it with . . . er . . . the end.

CHRIS: In other words, we'll be looking at the history of bottoms.

XAND: So, strap on your gas masks – it's time to examine the backside.

In Ancient Egypt, doctors specialised in different parts of the body, meaning that one unfortunate medic had the job title 'Shepherd of the Royal Bottom'. His job was to examine the king's poo and prescribe herbal remedies based on colour and texture. Let's hope he didn't take his work home with him.

These days, bottom doctors still exist, but they call themselves 'proctologists'.

XAND: Because it's less embarrassing at parties than calling yourself a bum shepherd.

CHRIS: If you ever see someone looking ill or distressed, you SHOULD offer to get them help or call an ambulance.

XAND: What you SHOULDN'T do is place them on the floor, turn them over and blow tobacco smoke up their bottom.

CHRIS: Yet this is exactly what someone in the eighteenth century would have done.

Although tobacco is now known to be very harmful, tobacco was thought to be good for you when it was introduced to Europe in the sixteenth century.

It was even used as medicine, which is where tobacco smoke enemas come in. To give one of these to someone, you'd stick a pair of bellows up their bottom and blow smoke into them. Blowing smoke up bottoms was used for headaches, colds, cramps and breathing problems. It was thought to be especially useful for victims of drowning – bellows were placed in emergency kits along the River Thames. If you saw someone flailing in the water, all you had to do was drag them out and waft some smoke up their rear end.

XAND: It would either make them better, or freak them out so much they'd pretend to be better so you'd go away.

At the start of the nineteenth century studies began to show that, far from being good for you, tobacco was actually poisonous, which might explain why smoke enemas fell out of fashion soon afterwards. Either that, or everyone realised how completely bonkers the whole thing was.

GROSS OUT

John Harvey Kellogg, who achieved fame as a manufacturer of breakfast cereals, was also a doctor who ran a health resort in America. One of the resort's treatments was squirting half a pint of yoghurt up a patient's bottom. While Kellogg's Corn Flakes caught on around the world, Kellogg's Yoghurt Surprise was, thankfully, less popular.

CHRIS: And it's not just smoke that has been sent into bottoms.

XAND: All sorts of liquids have been used for enemas.

CHRIS: People would then poo the liquid out again, thereby cleaning out their lower intestines.

XAND: Enemas are still used today to treat things like constipation, but back in the seventeenth century, they were used for pretty much everything.

A 'clyster' was a huge metal syringe with a nozzle at one end and a plunger at the other. A patient would get down on all fours and stick their bottom in the air, then a doctor would pop the nozzle . . . er, 'up', and release the liquid. This would usually be water, but sometimes it would have herbs and perfumes in. So at least it would smell nice on the way in.

King Louis XIV of France enjoyed enemas so much he had up to four a day, using a special royal clyster made from silver.

CHRIS: How apt that a king would choose to spend all day on the throne . . .

The tradition of enemas for general wellbeing lives on today, thanks to alternative medicine. There has even been a recent trend for coffee enemas, but many doctors think that these could actually be dangerous, as well as wasting a perfectly good drink. At any rate, it's bad manners to order one in a coffee shop.

XAND: I'm a little stuck about how to finish this section.

CHRIS: Keep pushing . . . I'm sure you'll get it out.

XAND: That's it! We can look at the history of constipation.

If you're having trouble plopping, your doctor might suggest foods that are high in fibre, like fruits, vegetables, nuts and bran cereals. What they won't do is tell you to eat mercury. Yet that's exactly what would have happened in the nineteenth century.

THE BOTTOM

We now know that the metal mercury is highly toxic, but in those days it was thought to cure everything. It was taken in pill form to cure constipation, especially on ships, where the fibre-free diets had everyone straining away whenever they tried to poo. The pills could, of course, give you serious mercury poisoning, but would at least take your mind off the constipation.

In 1893 Nikolai Tesla invented a machine called the 'violet ray generator' that consisted of a control box and an assortment of glowing glass tubes to stick on your body. Or to stick *up* your body, in the case of the one that cured constipation. But you had to be very careful when using it: if the fragile glass tube broke, constipation would be the least of your problems.

But even that looked inviting compared to the 'Recto Rotor'. Advertised in the mid-nineteenth century, this was a metal instrument that looked horribly like a drill attachment and went up your rear end. It doesn't seem to have caught on, which is hardly surprising. If the cure for constipation was to drill up your own bottom, it was probably better to live with constipation.

CHRIS: And that's it! Our journey through the history of medicine has come to an end.

XAND: I bet you're glad you live in the age of clean hospitals, scientific treatments and anaesthetic.

CHRIS: And not one of bloodletting, head drilling and smoke enemas.

XAND: But even in these days of safe treatment, getting sick is no fun, so take care of yourselves!

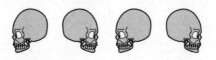

Asthma Attack

If someone has an asthma attack, get them to sit comfortably while you fetch their inhaler. If they don't have their inhaler with them, or it doesn't seem to help, find an adult or call 999.

Bleeding

If someone has a cut that's too big for a plaster, ask them to press on the wound with their hand, or use a towel or piece of clothing. This will help to slow down the bleeding. Get help from an adult, or call 999 if you think it's serious.

Broken Bones

If you think someone has broken a bone, tell them to keep their injury still and support it to stop it moving, using items such as clothes or cushions. Then find an adult or call 999.

Burns

To help someone with a burn, cool the area with cold, running water for at least ten minutes. When the burn has cooled, cover it with cling film or a

plastic bag to keep it clean. Call for an adult or call 999 if you think it's serious.

Choking

If someone's choking, hit them firmly on the back until they cough up whatever's causing the problem. If this doesn't work, call for an adult or call 999. Keep hitting them on the back until help arrives.

Collapse

If you find someone collapsed on the floor, find out if they're conscious by gently shaking their shoulders and speaking to them. If they don't respond but they're breathing, put them on their side with their head tipped back so their airway is open. Call 999 for an ambulance straight away.

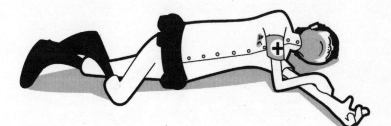

Turn the page for more amazing facts from Operation Ouch!

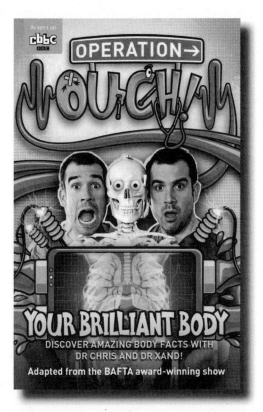

OPERATION OUCH!

Your Brilliant Body

Your Tongue

For its size, the tongue is the strongest muscle in the human body.

It's covered with about ten thousand taste buds and inside each of these there are up to one hundred cells helping you taste everything from the sweetest cake to the spiciest chilli.

Every time you eat or drink something, taste buds send messages to your brain about it. If it's an apple, your brain will probably tell you to go ahead and take a bite. If it's a raw onion, your brain will probably tell you to cook it first. Unless you like eating raw onions. Who are we to judge?

THAT'S BRILLIANT

Stephen Taylor from Coventry has the world's longest tongue. It measures ten centimetres from tip to lip, which means the whole thing is as long as a Cumberland sausage. It's so long he can even eat a yoghurt without using a spoon, which must save on the washing up.

Your sense of taste works closely with your sense of smell to determine overall flavour. This is why food sometimes tastes different when you have a cold – it's because your nose is blocked and doesn't work properly.

Tastes can be sweet, sour, salty, bitter or umami. Umami refers to the strong savoury flavour of foods like cheese, meat and fish. You could experience all these tastes at once if you made yourself a cheese and lemon sandwich covered with sugar, salt and vinegar. But don't. It would be disgusting.

Taste buds aren't just found on your tongue. They're also on the inside of your cheeks, the roof of your mouth and your lips. But wherever they are, you should be grateful to them. Without them, the tastiest sweets, the freshest fruits and the most delicious pizzas would all taste as horrible as the mouldy school dinner scrapings in the bins at the back of the playground.

DID YOU KNOW?

Hot chillies contain a substance called capsaicin. Capsaicin triggers the pain detectors on your tongue. This is why hot food sometimes gives you a burning sensation in your mouth. Some people avoid this painful experience at all costs, while others enjoy it and develop a taste for spicy foods.

XAND: As you get older, some of your taste buds die, and they are not replaced.

CHRIS: This means that younger people can be more sensitive to taste than older people.

XAND: Although that probably isn't a good enough excuse to leave the parts of your dinner you don't like.

DID YOU KNOW?

Your tongue print is as unique as your fingerprint. It's just as well the police chose fingerprints as the standard way to identify people, though. It wouldn't be very nice to have to dip your tongue in ink and lick a piece of paper.